From Paper Dolls to Perfume: My Story on Your Journey

By

Verlena O. Hawkins

Published by

Queen V Publishing
Englewood, Ohio
QueenVPublishing.com

Published by

Queen V Publishing
Englewood, Ohio
QueenVPublishing.com

Copyright ©2010 by Verlena O. Hawkins

All rights reserved. No part of this book may be reproduced or transmitted in any form or by any means, electronic or mechanical, without prior written consent of the Publisher, except for the inclusion of brief quotes in a review.

Queen V Publishing is a Christian contract publishing company of standard and integrity. We allow God's Word in you to do what it was sent to do for others.

Library of Congress Control Number: 2010928113

ISBN-13: 978-0-9817436-8-4

Cover design by Candace K.
Edited by Valerie J. Lewis Coleman of PenOfTheWriter.com and Tenita C. Johnson of SoItIsWritten.net

Printed in the United States of America

Dedication

I dedicate *From Paper Dolls to Perfume* to my parents—Willie Oliver, Jr. and Estella Baker Oliver—who guided me through the challenges of life.

Acknowledgements

So many have influenced my life that I cannot name them all however, I have to give mention as follows:
- My six sisters and brother: Thank you for a great childhood experience.
- Andre—my first born: Thank you for teaching me to stand up for myself.
- Juan—my second born: Thank you for treating me first class.
- Brandi—my daughter: Thank you for sharing your husband with me.
- Michael Dixon, Ja-Waan Hawkins and Rohan Tennie: I can't wait to see what great men you will become.
- Every uncle, aunt, cousin and friend: Thank you for protecting me and giving me forever to grow up.
- All my loved ones who await me on the other side: Thank you for teaching me about letting go of this life and embracing the next.
- Charlotte Carroway from Alaska who crowned me a poet after my first badly written poem.
- Every church that guided me in my walk with Christ: St. Paul AME Church of Ellabell, Georgia, Chapel 3 of South Korea, Cherryvale Baptist Church of South Carolina, New Life Bible Church of South Carolina, True Victory Baptist Church of North Pole, Alaska, Mt. Pisgah Baptist Church of Dayton, Ohio, Maranatha Christian Fellowship of Dayton, Ohio and Hillcrest Seven Day Adventist Church of Dayton, Ohio.
- To every group of Montgomery Development Center, Community Development Corporation Resource Consortium (CDCRC), Court Appointed Special Advocate (CASA) of Xenia, Women Aglow, Child

Evangelism Fellowship and *Walking in Victory* TV show: Thank you for empowering me to the next level.

- Last but not least, Tina Toles of Dayton Christian Writers Guild and Valerie J. Lewis Coleman of Pen of the Writer: Thank you for your publishing gifts and opportunities.

Table of Contents

Betrayal
Paper-Dolls Syndrome 12
Praying From a Distance 13
I Will Remember Your Pain 14
Your Journey Through Pain 15
Your Devastating Place 16
Wounded Trust 17
When Things Go Well With You, Remember Me 18

Healing and Encouragement
When Only Faith is Left 20
Believe God for the Best 21
Healed in the Hands of Jesus 22
Go On with Christ 23
You Can Make It 24
The Divine Power in You 25
I Still See Jesus 27
You Were Always There 28
Since You've Been Gone 29
My Home is Now a Haven 30

Unfaithfulness
Here We Are Again 32
When My Place is Given to Another 33
I Cry for Intimacy 34
If You Ever Need Someone 35
If Love is All It Takes 36
Giving You Back to God 37
I'm Not Hurting Anymore 38

Friendship

Just For You 40
Hello, Dear Friend 41
Are You Okay? 42
Why I Have Not Written 43
If I Called, Would You Answer? 44
The Mention of My Name 45
What Would It Mean to You? 46
What More Can I Do? 47
My Last Letter to You 48
Thank You for Forgiving Me 49
Good-Bye, Best Friend 50
A New Start 51

Sorrows

Precious Tears 53
A Song Among My Tears 54
Entrusted with Great Sorrows 55
When My Heart is Shaken 56
Silent Tears 57
I Thank God for You 58
Choice Perfume 59
About Verlena O. Hawkins 61

From Paper Dolls to Perfume

Betrayal

Verlena O. Hawkins
Paper-Dolls Syndrome

As an exciting young bride
    I waited for my prince to come take me away.
I thought the two of us
    would be happily married until this very day.
I loved and adored him
    yet I gave too much and the best of me
Because something strange
    was deeply brewing in his heart too dark to see.
My heart cried all the time
    for the intimacy I wanted and the love I had lost,
While my mind became fragile
    as I fearfully counted up the cost.
Leaving was not an option
    for little ole me as a paper-doll child
As I longed for the time
    of my cut-out dolls with their big cut-out smiles.
The paper dolls represented
    my innocent childish mind that refused to change.
They also represented
    the very best of me that I often blamed
For a lost friendship
    and a damaged marriage that wasn't meant to be,
As I learned the steps to letting go
    of the paper-doll syndrome to become the real me.

The key to change: Stop blaming and expecting others to make you happy. Change and create the new you whom you are capable of being.

From Paper Dolls to Perfume
Praying From a Distance

Although I really desire
    to be there at your side,
and speak sweet words of encouragement
    as you alone abide,
to lift your feeble hands
    and help you to pray,
I know that I can't,
    for I am now so far away.
Yet the many miles between us
    are not by chance.
In my absence, I'll be praying
    from a distance.

I'll thank Jesus for giving you
    a brand new day
And strength to get through it
    in a special way.
For though it gets hard sometimes,
    you are never alone.
He'll provide all that you'll ever need
    and the strength needed to go on.
For this is my joy concerning your trials
    and disturbing circumstances,
I can count it as a joy to be praying
    from a distance.

Verlena O. Hawkins
I Will Remember Your Pain

Every time I touch your heart, I will remember your pain
And the wounds that I have inflicted, hurting you once again.
I feel your anger and hurt, even a sense of distrust.
And I will take the full blame for whatever happens to us.
For it was not at all my intention to let my suspicions reign.
Yet my presumptions caused you so much pain.
I ask that you please forgive the hurt that I've done to you.
And allow Jesus to heal you, and make your life anew.
I don't ask for that special place I unknowingly destroyed,
Which left you feeling devastated, lonely and with a void.
But I ask that you go on with life and be restored and healed.
For this is the only eternal token that what we had was real.
So I say my good-bye, as life will never be the same.
And every time I touch your heart, I'll remember your pain.

From Paper Dolls to Perfume
Your Journey Through Pain

I don't understand the pain
That you're going through.
Neither do I know what to say,
Nor what to do.
But I want you to know
You're the Master of this pain.
And I'm just a student here,
With knowledge to gain.
I'll cry because you cry
When the pain gets bad.
I'll let you talk when needed
About times that are sad.
Since I never walked
This particular road before,
I'll let you do the leading
To unlock each new door.
I won't tell you how to feel,
For this journey is not mine;
You'll discover the healing
That comes in God's time.

Verlena O. Hawkins
Your Devastating Place

While you are at your devastating place
on your journey home,
remember that God is there with you
and that He'll never leave you alone.
Even though someone has called the ambulance
and help is on the way,
The Angelic Host is now hard at work,
on your case especially today.
They are carrying out the orders they have had
before the beginning of time,
directing your footsteps in line with scripture
and directing your life to be divine.
My what lessons you are going to learn
from this terrible pain!
And oh what leaps and bounds you will grow
on your journey to being normal again.
What a testimony you will have to share
concerning your trail of tears,
while telling of God's daily faithfulness
and goodness all these years!
So as you are at your devastating place
on your journey home,
remember that God is there with you
and that he'll never leave you alone.

From Paper Dolls to Perfume
Wounded Trust

I'm sorry for your wounded trust
and the things I didn't understand;
for how my angry words damaged you
when you needed a helping hand.
I didn't say those things to hurt
I just didn't know how to help you.
And every time you failed yourself,
my praises became few.
I didn't understand the steep mountain
nor your laborious struggle,
until my eyes were opened
and an explanation was given by another.
No one can understand your journey,
unless he's walked in your shoes.
No one can understand your failure,
unless they've seen your tools.
So I'd like to say that with God's help
you can make it to the top.
And I'll be there to help you;
I'll be your solid rock.
And maybe one day very soon,
healthy trust will replace wounded trust
so that you can be restored
and catch up with the rest of us.

Verlena O. Hawkins

When Things Go Well With You, Remember Me

When things go well with you, remember me.
Remember my goals in life and what I had hoped to be.
Remember the agony and pain that I am going through.
Remember me in this place; not doing what I want to do.
Remember me the way I was before this terrible thing;
when I would worship, serve, pray and sing.

When things go well with you, remember family and friends.
Remember their sorrow and pain that seem to have no end!
Remember their financial needs and spiritual ones too.
Ask God how you can help; show you what to do.
You have so many resources that have been overlooked.
God can use each one of them like a bubbling brook.

When things go well with you, declare God's Word to me.
Call forth things that are not as they ought to be.
Remember that all things will work together for good;
and His Word toward me will accomplish what it should.

When things go well with you, please remember me…
That this trial will cause me to be the best I can be.

Healing and Encouragement

Verlena O. Hawkins
When Only Faith is Left

So many of my friends marvel at what I'm going through.
And how I find joy and strength to do the things that I do.
My road of suffering has been paved with so much pain,
   But the Lord has restored me over and over again.
   I know that you are proud of me; I'm proud of myself.
   But what am I supposed to do when only faith is left?

You all have been my strength; more than you'll ever know,
   By sending cards and letters when I got emotionally low.
   Reassuring and telling me that I will never be alone.
   For I'm just a traveler here; Heaven is my home.
   So I'll cling to Jesus—my Rock—who's in the cleft.
   What am I supposed to do when only faith is left?

I thank God also for the Holy Spirit, my stay-with friend.
He has always been with me and will be to the end.
He has comforted me when healing my wounds each time.
Reminding me that no matter what; I am His and He is mine.
He handles my tears so carefully as He puts them on a shelf.
For that is how one acts when only faith is left.

From Paper Dolls to Perfume
Believe God for the Best

Although your plans did not work out today
And you're hindered from doing what you wanted to,
Remember to let Him have His way,
Allowing Him freedom in what He wants to do.

As He takes you from glory to glory,
By allowing crisis in your life to test.
Whether you will tell the old, old story
As you just believe God for the best.

In all your ways, acknowledge Him
And He will direct your path, it's true.
You must believe that He will not condemn,
For He really wants what's best for you, too.

Trust in Him with all your heart
As He brings you into His perfect rest.
Trust and obey; that's your part,
As you believe God for the best.

Verlena O. Hawkins
Healed in the Hands of Jesus

May you be healed in the hands of Jesus as you bravely embrace your pain today.

Feel Christ's love, in which you can trust, for He is still the only way.

May you feel His love and know also that He cares for you.

He is the only one on whom you can depend. His strength and courage will pull you through.

May you rest in His comfort and get healing for your soul, knowing deep in your heart, there is no other way.

When you accept salvation, then you can go on your journey and start this glorious day.

May you be healed in the hands of Jesus, since that is where you are this day.

He is more than a healer; He's a Savior you can trust. But my question to you is: Will you accept Him today?

From Paper Dolls to Perfume
Go On with Christ

When you are released from your marriage vows,
from the daily crosses, the battles and trials;
from the abusive scorn each and every day
to a new divine pathway where you won't stray.

Go on bravely through that valley of death
to the arms of Jesus, whom you've loved the best.
Know that He's beside you and has paid the price
take that fearful leap and go on with Christ.

When your last prayer is "Lord, my marriage, save!"
Yet being put away, after all you gave.
Know that you can't control another person's free will
in a marriage with no joy, hopes or thrills.

Striving by God's power to keep yourself alive
Amidst so much confusion when the enemy abides.
Know that there's much living after married life.
Take that fearful leap and go on with Christ.

Verlena O. Hawkins
You Can Make It

The road that you're traveling has been very hard.
The load that you're carrying seems oh so large.
The strain is now showing on your lovely face,
      while your steady footsteps seem to lose pace.
So take time from your worrying and start worshipping.
For you have left your first love.
Distracted by problems that you must now admit.
      But by getting closer to Christ, you can make it.
Submit that home to the almighty God in every single prayer.
Knowing He'll never leave you for He's always there.
Bring all of the many concerns of your children, too.
      He has a path for their lives and much for them to do.
Stop wrestling with the situation and start resting in Christ.
He is aware of your turmoil having already paid the price.
Focus on His sovereign will; His fellowship never omit.
      Since He is the Lily of your valley, you can make it!

From Paper Dolls to Perfume
The Divine Power in You

It's okay my dear friend,
    if you don't want to talk.
I feel your crippling hurt;
    I see your staggering walk.
Weak from a devastating battle
    that wasn't committed to God;
Fleeing from a defeating enemy
    when the situation got hard.
Out-of-control fretting
    and focusing on faults;
Worshipping your problems
    with negative thoughts.
By neglecting God's Word
    and not knowing what to do,
You failed to use your abilities
    and the divine power in you.
Divine power has been given
    to demolish strongholds.
From treasures that are deep
    to riches untold.
You can take captive anything
    that exalts itself against God,
And rise above the situations
    when times get hard.
By bringing every thought captive
    to the power of Christ,
You are a child of the King,
    so don't even think twice.
Destroy every disobedience
    and do what God says do.
For you are using your abilities

Verlena O. Hawkins
and the divine power in you.
As you obey God's plan,
    Remember healing is a choice.
With love and forgiveness,
    you can choose to rejoice.
And the problem that you thought
    you had with them,
That energy can be focused on Christ
    and bring glory to Him.
You are no longer a victim,
    for you've learned to overcome
And you now seek God's approval,
    and that His will to be done.
So as you look back triumphantly
    on all you've been through,
Continue to yield to the Holy Spirit,
    the divine power in you.

From Paper Dolls to Perfume
I Still See Jesus

I often see you struggling under a load of care.
I also see Jesus helping you with the burdens you must bear.
Though you have now become so weary, worn and tired,
You are still an overcomer which is to be admired.

No matter how bad things get, you keep pressing on.
And I can still see Jesus there, for you are never alone.
He is always there to comfort when you feel you're through,
Empowering you for the many things you must still endure.

Whatever you are going through please don't ever give up.
Jesus is there to help you drink from life's bitter cup.

Verlena O. Hawkins
You Were Always There

You were always there for little ol' lonely me;
Helping me to be the very best that I could ever be.
Many times I really didn't understand
That your way of showing love was lending a helping hand.
We had many hard times, but with love, made it through.
And today dear friend, I want to show how much I appreciate you.
You were always there with a kind word and a lovely smile,
not realizing that ministering to me might take you awhile.

But somehow that never bothered or concerned you
Because you realized that you had an important job to do.
That job was to help me and bring me to this end.
And because of your hard work you grew to be my friend.

You were always there for me and now I'm here for you;
To love, encourage and see you through.
Making your day a little sweeter and a bit brighter;
Helping you carry your burdens to make your load lighter.
I want you to know with all my heart that I do care.
And I'm here for you today because yesterday you were there.

From Paper Dolls to Perfume
Since You've Been Gone

Since you've been gone
    from our presence and home,
    we are learning to let go
    and move on.

Sometimes we still go to the phone,
    waiting to call your name,
    but you are not there anymore
    everything has changed.

You have moved from by our sides
    to deep within our hearts,
    where we don't have to fear you leaving
    or fear you abandoning our hearts.

And though it gets hard sometimes
    because we feel so alone
    Jesus gives us the strength we need
    to be content and move on.

Verlena O. Hawkins
My Home is Now a Haven

My home is now a haven
for God's people to rest.
He picks each one of them,
for He alone knows best.
They know that they are welcomed
and stay as long as they need,
as we worship God together
for His divine deeds.

My home is now a haven;
a place of joy and peace.
Sometimes it's a resting place
until a battle's ceased.
It's a place where we can laugh
Or cry, if we must,
but always in God's presence is
where there's comfort for us.

My home is now a haven
after many years of dreams
which I thought would never come to pass,
for that was the way it seemed;
Now the windows of Heaven have opened
for weary travelers to rest.
My home is now a haven,
a place where they can nest.

From Paper Dolls to Perfume

Unfaithfulness

Verlena O. Hawkins
Here We Are Again

Here we are once again
at the place of so much pain,
abandoning each other once more
by letting silence reign.

We have gone through this before
and I choose to give a Godly reaction,
for all this unnecessary neglect
and threats of a divorce action.

God is still the lifter of my head
and in Him I put my total trust.
Not in your selfish personal opinions
of what is best for us.

Just because I want to be loved
and you don't have the time
doesn't mean that I will jump this ship
to give up years of what is mine.

This marriage is Jesus' marriage;
I'm only a card to be played.
He knows the game from the beginning
and He knows where I should be laid.

No more fretting and crying for me;
at His throne I'll lay.
I'm tired of these heavy loads
as I bear my crosses each day.

So here we are once again
at the place of so much pain
And while I walk through it this time,
I choose to give Him praise.

From Paper Dolls to Perfume
When My Place is Given to Another

When my wifely place
is given to another,
when I am committed
to forsake all others,
what do I, as a prayerful
woman of God, do?
How do I remain pure,
faithful and true
when I have finally lost
my once best friend?
How do I journey on
to my expected end?
How do I fight strategically
these batteries of trials,
which happened to come along
with my marriage vows?
I do it by choice and commitment
to a God whom I can trust;
and I do whatever it takes,
taking whatever I must.
I stay absolutely focused
on the one true God,
having already been empowered
for when times get hard.
When my wifely place
is given to another,
I remember that I am called
to forsake all others.

Verlena O. Hawkins
I Cry for Intimacy

I cry for intimacy in a marriage grown cold.

I cry for intimacy with a spouse who's old.

I cry for intimacy with each fleeing day.

I cry for intimacy in a starving new way.

I cry for intimacy while being put on hold.

I cry for intimacy like a news breaking story untold.

I cry for intimacy among his so called friends.

I cry for intimacy on a lonely journey that doesn't end.

I cry for intimacy.

From Paper Dolls to Perfume
If You Ever Need Someone

If you ever need someone
to be there for you,
someone who really cares,
someone capable of bringing you through.
If you ever need someone
in the lonely midnight hour,
I will always be there praying,
with God's divine power.
If you ever need someone
who chooses to share your life,
remember that I am here at home,
waiting to be your wife.
If you ever need someone
after chasing empty dreams,
I will receive you with all my love
in a marriage that God has redeemed.
If you ever need someone
who is committed as can be,
don't look any further my darling,
come on home to me.

Verlena O. Hawkins
If Love is All It Takes

If love is all it takes to show you how much I care,
why are you not here, but in the streets somewhere?

If love is all it takes to ease the hurts and pains,
why are you still wandering in confusion as though there's no love to gain?

If love is all it takes to break down your walls of defense,
why are you sitting in silence, when silence makes no sense?

If love is all it takes to show you a better way,
why are you still doing your own thing and going astray?

If love is all it takes to teach you my child,
why are you still unlearned behind that false smile?

If love is all it takes to have bring you home to me,
then why are you still fighting to be free?

From Paper Dolls to Perfume
Giving You Back to God

I have been crying and worrying because your heart's become hard, but starting this very day, I'm giving you back to God.

You were only lent to me for a short season and I've tried to take care of you for this very reason.

But sometimes, situations with people can turn out so odd. That's why I'm not giving up on you, I'm giving you back to God.

I know you can't see it now, but I'm doing my very best to guide and gently equip you to someday leave this nest.

But you must do your part to try and understand that all I want for you dear is God's most perfect plan.

That is the reason why letting go is so hard, but I'll find the strength I need for I'm giving you back to God.

Now there is one special thing that I want you to know. I love you with all my heart as I finally let you go.

And if you should ever need me, I'll only be a prayer away, listening and looking for your love in each new passing day.

Believing that I made the best decision by using the chastening rod and since nothing else seemed to work I'm giving you back to God.

Verlena O. Hawkins

I'm Not Hurting Anymore

I know that you must be wondering
what has happened to me,
with all the hurt and anguish
that has been killing the real me.
I've died in so many ways,
but this time, it's in Christ,
who has helped me all these years
by paying the sacrificial price.
I've died to ever needing anyone
to be the living God for me
and I'll always be indebted to Christ
for finally setting me free.
I've died to loneliness and neediness
and desiring another's touch,
for Christ holds me so ever near Him
and He loves me so much.
I've died to changing myself for others;
Christ's glory now shines through me,
and it will change and transform me
into what I am destined to be.
I just wanted to let you know today
that I'm not hurting anymore,
for the hurt has broken years of chains,
pointing me to Heaven's door.
The enemy has planned all these hurts
to cripple and disarm me,
but Christ has turned it around for my own good
and I'm not hurting anymore – I'm free.

From Paper Dolls to Perfume

Friendship

Verlena O. Hawkins
Just For You

Look what God is doing now
            just for you.
How He is giving you strength
            to bring you through.
He has given you living hope
            in the lonely night
until your faith is manifested,
            and it becomes sight.
You are learning who He is
            and loving Him so,
As you learn His character
            And Him you get to know.
He imparts wisdom into you
            on your sick bed,
as He changes your heart
            and your worried head.
He wants to show you especially
            what He can do
and that He cannot only do it for others, but do it also,
            just for you.

From Paper Dolls to Perfume
Hello, Dear Friend

Hello, dear friend of this heart of mine.
How in the world are you?
How is your work and the things you've been called to do?
How are the children these days?
I know that they've grown and have probably left out on their own.
How is your darling and loving mate—your daily best friend?
And the love that you share with each other for there seems to be no end?

I so often think of you in my heart,
with pure love and many smiles.
I wonder what you are going through
among life's many trials.
I wonder if you ever think of me
as I so often think of you;
realizing how busy you must be daily
with everything you have to do.

Yet it is so sad how we don't keep in touch
to reminisce about God's love
and encourage each other in Christ,
concerning things below and above.
I want you to know that just today
I'm thinking of you again
and if I could speak with you once more,
I would say "Hello, dear friend."

Verlena O. Hawkins

Are You Okay?

Hi, dear friend, I just stopped by
to see if you were okay.
I have heard of the awful trial,
which has overshadowed your way.

I realize that we are not as close
as we used to be,
and I take full responsibility for it.
Put the blame on me.

All of that does not matter now,
for I am concerned about your pain.
I know there's nothing I can do or say
as this terrible situation reigns.

I won't lecture you this time
or remind you about what Scriptures say.
I'll just demonstrate Christ's love to you
and do it in a biblical way.

I am crying tonight because in my heart,
I feel you too are crying within.
And no matter what has happened in the past,
I still feel that deepness of kin.

I don't mean to take up your time,
or to go on this way.
I just wanted to ask from my heart to yours,
"Are you okay?"

From Paper Dolls to Perfume
Why I Have Not Written

You must be wondering by now
why I have not written,
when I know that your heart is broken
and perhaps even smitten.
But I'm giving you time to recover
from our bad ordeal
so that you can test our friendship
to know whether it's real.
I can't take back the terrible pain
that I have caused you
and there are no words to say
or anything that I can do.
But I do want you to know for sure
that wasn't my heart's desire,
for you are one of my dearest friends,
one that I really admire.
I know you feel I wasn't compassionate
while using the chastening rod,
but I really did try to be merciful,
for confronting you was hard.

Verlena O. Hawkins
If I Called, Would You Answer?

If I called, would you answer me and hear my deepest plea?

If I were wounded and remembered you, would you call to see about me?

If I asked you to forgive all the pain I have caused you,

if my cry came to your attentive ear what would you choose to do?

If I drew a word picture of the things I didn't really understand; if I shared with you all of my fears, would you hold my trembling hand?

If I explained my thoughts to you of your friendship I feared to lose, would you give up this friendship of ours just because it was yours to choose?

If I called, would you answer and hear my deepest plea?

If I were wounded and remembered you, would you call to see about me?

From Paper Dolls to Perfume
The Mention of My Name

I'm sorry that the mention of my name has hurt you again, and that so many memories of me have stirred up your pain.

My desire is for you to be healed and remember what we had and how we used to have so much fun before everything went bad.

Remember the times we used to play and sing in the spring; remember all of the joy and happiness that meeting each other would bring.

Remember how we corrected each other and then we went on to grow; we were better because of our friendship and in our character, it did show.

So why have we let this last incident come between the two of us? And why are we acting like we are unsure and afraid to trust?

We know each other's strengths and weaknesses, each other's failures and faults. We know the purity of each other's heart or at least we ought.

I hope that we will have mutual respect for what was full and free, knowing that whether this relationship grows depends upon you and me.

And when you hear my name the next time, you will experience joy again. And when I hear the name of my best friend, I will feel the same.

Verlena O. Hawkins
What Would It Mean to You?

What would it mean to you
    if I no longer did the things
    that I now do?
What would it mean to you
    if I no longer showed
    my love toward you?
What would it mean to you
    if I stopped writing about you
    in all of my poems?
What would it mean to you
    if I should choose
    to leave you alone?
What would it mean to you?
    Did you ever think that
    I might not be here?
What would it mean to you
    if you never heard
    from me this year?

From Paper Dolls to Perfume
What More Can I Do?

What more can I say to you
than I have said yesterday?
How much repenting can I do
or what price can I pay?
How many sorrowful tears must I cry
to show you that I really care?
How heavy must my burden get
that I must everyday bear?
How many times must I show I'm sorry
before you are ever healed?
How long must my heart bleed within
before believing my repentance is real?
How long must this lack of reconciliation go on
proving how bad I have hurt you?
Name your price for our restoration.
Let me know what more I can do.

Verlena O. Hawkins
My Last Letter to You

My last letter to you doesn't mean
that I do not love you.
It only means that I respect your choice
to do what you've chosen to do.
My last letter to you doesn't mean
that I no longer care.
It only means that sometimes friendships end,
because life isn't always fair.
My last letter to you doesn't mean
that you alone are to blame,
or that the admiration I have for you
will ever, ever change.
My last letter to you doesn't mean
that I don't accept the part I played
which cost the both of us this relationship;
the highest price we paid.
My last letter to you doesn't mean
that I do not love you.
It only means that I respect your choice
to do what you've chosen to do.

From Paper Dolls to Perfume
Thank You for Forgiving Me

Thank you for finally forgiving me
for the wrong that I have done.
Even though you don't feel like it,
the feeling will one day come.
Thank you for choosing to set me free
from the hurt that I put you in.
Even though our relationship will never be the same,
neither will we be that close again.
Thank you for choosing to love me once more
as you still struggle on your way.
And may I one day return the special favor
even if it's not today.
Thank you for also reassuring me
that deep down inside you care,
and if I ever wanted to reach out to you
you would always be there.

Verlena O. Hawkins
Good-Bye, Best Friend

Do you feel this separating pull and tug going on between you and I? Although neither of us wants to let go, it's inevitable that we can't deny.

We have done all that our friendship was meant to do and it's been fun. But we must let go and say good-bye, for our traveling together is done.

We started out on a busy path together, total strangers journeying to the end. And somewhere along the way, the Lord called us to be best friends.

Oh my, did we have a grand old time; enjoying what the Lord gave. Never realizing that He would call us apart to a different road to pave.

One thing that I am going to miss dearly about being your best friend is the special love that I thought we had, one that would never end.

But it will, like so many of my other best friends in the past. First, we will forsake our special friendship and then the memories will fade fast.

And there will come a time when we no longer mention each other's name because of the miles, the years and the different paths that we each claimed.

It's no one's fault, for this friendship came with no guaranteed papers or reasons. It was just a treasure verses a jewel, lent to us for a season.

So today I say, "Good-bye my best friend." With warm streaming tears I say, Good-bye." I won't be lonely, for the separation has been gradual as the time went by.

But I shed these tears because of things that I thought would never end. It will and we both know it, so I'll say, "Good-bye best friend."

From Paper Dolls to Perfume
A New Start

We must let go to begin a new start.
But we'll always be close to each other's heart.
I can't embrace something that is so very new,
unless I am willing to let go of you.
You too must have an opportunity to move on and grow,
and you also must release me and let me go,
that we might discover what God has for us.
And we will discover it, for it is a must.
So, as we go from one stage to another,
remember He has called you to walk as my brother.
So let's love one another, which is God's command.
Binding hearts together and letting go of each other's hand,
crying, if we must, for in sweetness we must depart.
We have to let go and begin a new start.

Verlena O. Hawkins

Sorrows

From Paper Dolls to Perfume
Precious Tears

Oh, precious tears that flow so free
What is so wrong? What could it be
That suddenly causes you to overflow?
Tell me please, I want to know.
Whatever it is don't ever lose hope.
God will provide strength for you to cope.

Oh, precious tears that flow so free
This thing is not permanent as you will see.
It's only to test your faith in God
Who molds your character as life gets hard.
He'll restore you in the fullness of time
Saying, "I am His and He is mine."

Oh, precious tears that flow so free
Don't get caught up in what might be.
Focus on who is and coming again
It's Jesus the Christ—our friend from within.
He was there before when things got hard
And He'll be there again for He's the living God.

Verlena O. Hawkins

A Song Among My Tears

Lord, as I sing about Your goodness
In a song among my tears,
I have lightning-flash remembrances
Of Your goodness of former years.
My tears are not tears of sadness
Neither of sorrow and woe,
But they are tears of triumphant joy
Of where I am and where I'll go.
It's a glorious song of jubilation, Lord,
That I sing unto You
One of adoration and magnificent praise
Of the miracles that You do.
A song of Your soon-coming visit
To take Your child home
For though I don't always feel Your presence
You have never left me alone.
And whether You choose to come today
Or return in future years,
I'll keep right on singing to You, Lord,
With a song among my tears.

From Paper Dolls to Perfume
Entrusted with Great Sorrows

God has entrusted us with such great
Overwhelming sorrows
That blind and shatter our dreams
For happy tomorrows.
They will steal our loving memories
Of so many yesterdays
And add enormous fear to our future
In brand new ways.
But we must always focus on God
And not all the problems
For truly He is omnipotent
And certainly He can solve them.
Remembering that He knows how much
Each of us can bear,
And no matter how bad situations get
He keeps us in His care.
Joining in the fellowship of His suffering
Brings glory to His name
Which produces godly character
Instead of so much shame.
So as you think of the great sorrows
Entrusted to you
Seek God on how to use them
For His glory as He brings you through.

Verlena O. Hawkins
When My Heart is Shaken

When trouble comes in my home
And grips everyone with fear;
When peace flees and I'm all alone
I'll run to my God who's near.

When my confidence slips away and strays
And my mind can't keep calm within,
I'll find my Bible and start on my way
And meet You in our secret place, friend.

The only answer is in Your Word alone
And I'm learning to keep it near
To comfort my troubled heart
And to dry each fearful tear.

From Paper Dolls to Perfume
Silent Tears

Silent tears, lonely tears
Where are you coming from?
From a mind that can't grasp
Yet refuses to run.

Silent tears, lonely tears
What are your plans?
To stay close by my Master's side
And cling to His hands.

Silent tears, lonely tears
Aren't you afraid?
Not really, by His stripes I'm healed
And the price has been paid.

Silent tears, lonely tears
Where have you gone?
Nowhere, for I've been given permission
To just cry and cry alone.

Verlena O. Hawkins
I Thank God for You

It has been quite a while now
    since God almost called you home.
And oh how my life would have been empty,
    if you would have gone.
I thank God for how He spared your life
    by giving you back to us.
I thank Him for how He dealt with me,
    for He taught me how to trust.
He has even done a mighty work in you
    since that terrible time.
And you have learned to walk with Him
    in the body and the mind.
So today, I thank God for the experience
    of what He has done for you.
And I thank Him for His divine plan
    of what He is still going to do.

From Paper Dolls to Perfume
Choice Perfume

I didn't know what God was doing
when He allowed turmoil in my life.
These trials seemingly came from everywhere;
my life was filled with strife.
I was like a crushed and damaged fruit,
trodden and trampled on by men.
So I thought I should examine myself
to see if I had sinned.
I had an ocean of swift, flowing tears
with a bruised heart to match;
my broken spirit was grieved daily,
in the Earth, there was no patch.
I thought this process would never end
for it had gone on so long.
In my hurt I blamed God,
thinking that He was wrong
for allowing me to always go through
such awful pain and tears.
Neither could I see any reason
for suffering all these years.
But God had put my life in a vat,
pressing out evil and putting in good,
and lining my life up with Scripture
like no one else could.
Now I understand the reason why
I had gone through such gloom;
God was preparing my shaken life
to be choice perfume.

Verlena O. Hawkins

My Story on Your Journey

Reflect on your journey and capture your thoughts below:

_____
_____
_____
_____
_____
_____
_____
_____
_____
_____
_____
_____
_____
_____
_____
_____
_____
_____
_____
_____
_____
_____
_____

About Verlena O. Hawkins

As an advocate for children, Verlena O. Hawkins has fourteen years of experience with foster care and mental health. She is a financial-literacy counselor, speaker and facilitator for women groups. Her passion is sending cards to encourage women on difficult journeys. Verlena graduated from Sinclair Community College with a mental health degree and Capital University with a degree in social work.

Verlena O. Hawkins
Queen V Publishing
The Doorway to YOUR Destiny!

Go thou and publish abroad the kingdom of God.
—Luke 9:60

We are a Christian contract publisher committed to transforming manuscripts into polished works of art. **Queen V Publishing**, a company of standard and integrity, offers an alternative that allows God's word in YOU to do what it was sent to do for OTHERS.

Visit the website for complete guidelines on manuscript submission and the plan that best fits your literary goals.

QueenVPublishing.com
We help experts master self-publishing!

Valerie J. Lewis Coleman
Englewood, Ohio
888.802.1802
Info@penofthewriter.com

Pen of the Writer
Taking writers from pen to paper to published!

*Out of Ephraim was there a root of them against Amalek; after thee, Benjamin, among thy people; out of Machir came down governors, and out of Zebulun they that handle the **pen of the writer**.*
—Judges 5:14

P_{en} O_{f the} W_{rit}ER
A Christian publishing company committed to using the writing pen as a weapon to fight the enemy and celebrate the good news of Christ Jesus.

When I See Me™ BIPOC Children's Book Fair
(WhenISeeMe.com)
Book publishing
Writing workshops
Mentoring

Pen of the Writer, LLC
Englewood, Ohio
888.802.1802
PenOfTheWriter.com
info@penofthewriter.com

Verlena O. Hawkins
For speaking engagements or to order additional copies of

From Paper Dolls to Perfume

Verlena O. Hawkins
vhawkins@gatewaycsb.org

* * * * * * * * * * * * * * * * * *

Please mail _____ copies of

From Paper Dolls to Perfume

_____
Name

_____
Address

_____
City / State / Zip

(_____)_____
Phone

_____
Email

Quantity	Price Per Book	Total
	$9.95	
Sales Tax (Georgia residents add $0.40 per book)		
Shipping ($3.99 first book, $0.99 each additional)		
Grand Total* (Payable to: Verlena O. Hawkins)		

* Certified check and money orders only

www.ingramcontent.com/pod-product-compliance
Lightning Source LLC
Chambersburg PA
CBHW072109290426
44110CB00014B/1880